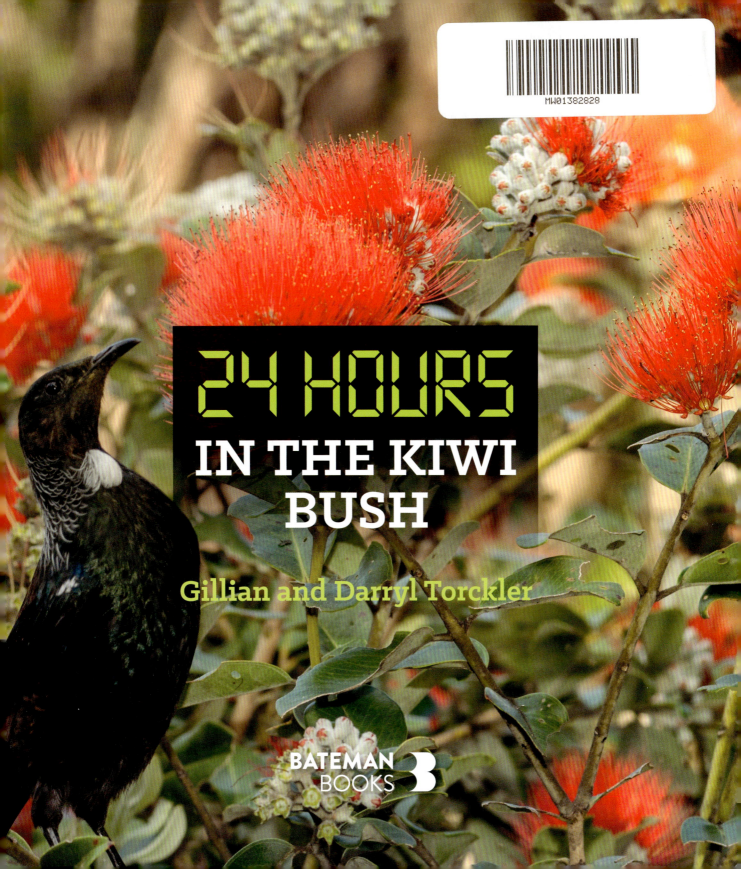

24 HOURS
IN THE KIWI BUSH

Gillian and Darryl Torckler

BATEMAN BOOKS

Introduction

We usually visit the New Zealand bush in daylight hours. Our footsteps disturb insects and quick-moving fantails swoop in to capture those that are trying to get out of our way. Some only escape for a moment before the energetic fantails grab them. Scraping the leaf litter away with our boots sends beetles and centipedes scattering. They are keen to avoid the light and the potential predator that has disturbed their home.

Before the summer sun has risen, birds fill the air with birdsong. Once this morning chorus dies away, the hum of newly hatched cicadas takes over. Soon busy bees add their own buzz as they move from flower to flower. But so much of the life of the forest remains unseen. Many animals spend their entire lives underground, like cicada nymphs before they hatch. Some animals, like the grub of the huhu beetle, spend their lives deep inside tree trunks.

Many animals are only active at night and are rarely seen during the day. Night-time is when the bush really comes alive — it's the time when many of the insects and reptiles are most active. Night-time is also a dangerous time. Hungry spiders, wētā and ruru are hunting. But night-time is also transformation time. Many creatures use the cover of darkness to emerge with wings for the first time — like the pūriri moth and the cicada.

As interesting as the night is, it is the daytime activity that keeps the trees and the animals alive. Birds and bees spread pollen as they move about the flowers. Other birds eat berries and seeds that they then spread far and wide in their droppings. These birds are essential to the life cycle of the bush.

Every 24 hours in the bush, the same pattern is observed. Day turns to night and night turns back to day. Life in the trees and in the air and underground never stops. The animals that live in the bush have adapted to their conditions and to living alongside each other. For many, every day is a struggle to survive. There are many natural predators. And this was in perfect balance until new predators were introduced. Our New Zealand wildlife, especially our birds, had not learned to adapt or defend themselves against fast moving and aggressive predators like rats, stoats and ferrets. Even domestic cats attack young birds and introduced possums take eggs from nests. Many New Zealand birds are now extinct or under threat. But luckily some are also recovering too.

New Zealand's native bush is very accessible and easily explored. In this book we share some of the birds, insects and animals we've encountered. We share what we have seen and what scientists have learned about their lifestyle. Life in the bush is always interesting.

Moonlight is filtered by the canopy of tall trees. The light barely reaches the ground where a **wētā** searches for food. Leaves rustle as a heavier animal comes close. The wētā stops eating. It senses a dark shadow above and takes no chances. It leaps out of the way to safety. Its mate is not so lucky and is caught by a **nursery-web spider** that pounces just in time.

Under the cover of darkness, **tree wētā** munch on leaves, berries, seeds, flowers, lichen and small creatures they come across. A **moth** lands on a branch nearby. It has been flying through the tree-tops looking for a mate. So far, the moth has avoided flying into the webs that spiders have been busy building between tree branches in order to catch their unsuspecting prey.

One insect hasn't been so lucky, becoming trapped by the sticky filaments. Spider webs are hard to see in the dark night, but tonight the tiny filaments of the web are glistening with dew in the moonlight. Nearby a pair of native **cockroaches** have avoided the sticky web, but found each other.

These nocturnal insects have luckily survived another busy night in the bush. After a successful night, wētā crawl into tree hollows. They will hide there, away from predators, until the cover of darkness returns. Then their night-time scavenging will begin all over again.

00:00 – 04:00

Wētā

Wētā are often feared by people, but there really is nothing to be afraid of. They do bite when frightened but rarely bite people. Wētā are related to grasshoppers and there are over 80 different species in New Zealand that fall into five main types — tree, ground, tusked, cave and giant wētā. Wētā really stink. That is how their worst enemies, rats, find them. Rats and other pests have feasted on wētā to near extinction. But the wētā continue to survive by laying batches of eggs, ten at a time, over the winter months. A female wētā may lay ten batches of eggs over the winter, but they need that many because the small wētā struggle to survive against bigger predators. Those that do survive shed their outer skin (moult) ten or more times before they reach adult size. All wētā are nocturnal scavengers. They eat plants, fungi, leaves, seeds, fruit and dead insects.

FUN FACT Wētā is a Māori word that means 'god of all ugly things' and many people would agree with that. Even the scientific name, *Deinacrida*, means 'terrible grasshopper'.

Orb-web spider

There are over 2000 different species of spider in New Zealand. But as you walk through the bush you are more likely to see, or even walk into, a web than you are to see the spider who built it. Web-building spiders rely on winds to help them spread the silk threads between trees. They start their webs with the long radial lines first. Then they work around the radial lines, from the outer edge to the inner edge, filling in the shorter lines in between. Once the web is completed, they wait at the centre ready to attack any insects that stray inside. They rely on these webs to catch insects, which become stuck to the sticky strands of silk.

FUN FACT Spiders spin silk threads that they use to hang in mid-air. They glide on these long threads with the wind. Sometimes, the wind takes them far away from their forest home — into the atmosphere and out to sea.

Nursery-web spider

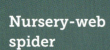

FUN FACT Spiders moult, or shed their skin, as they grow, and they do this up to six times before they reach their adult size.

Unlike other spiders, the nusery-web spider is a wanderer. Nursery-web spiders build dense webs but not to catch food. They build complex shapes to protect their eggs and baby spiders. You will often see their webs attached to gorse bushes. These wandering spiders are nocturnal hunters that search out, stalk and pounce on their prey. Typically, they seek out small insects, larvae and ground-living animals such as worms.

Moths | Pēpepe

There are less than 30 native butterflies in New Zealand, but thousands of different moths. Typically, moths are active at night and butterflies during the day. Most moths, like butterflies, start their lives as caterpillars and are encased in a cocoon before they become moths. Adult moths live for only a few days once they emerge from their cocoon. So their nights are filled with gathering nectar from bush plants before finding a mate. Moths spread pollen as they visit different plants and flowers during their short flying lives.

FUN FACT Some female moths are flightless and attract male moths by releasing a strong scent.

Is it a moth or a butterfly?

	Moth	Butterfly
Active time	Night	Day
Body	Round	Flat
Wing position at rest	Spread out	Held upright and together
Colour	Dull, earthy tones	Bright

Native bush cockroach | Kokoroihe

There are thousands of cockroach species around the world, and although many people shy away from them, these bush cockroaches are an essential part of the bush ecology. These are different from the ones that people dread entering their houses, which are typically larger and imported. There are 10–20 native cockroach species that are active at night and hide in dark crevices in the forest during the day.

FUN FACT Cockroaches are bush recyclers. They eat and break down organic matter that ultimately becomes the compost that plants grow in.

After a gruelling 60-minute climb from the soil below, a **cicada** has emerged from its shell. Its wet wings are spread wide to dry in the night air. Its wings will not be dry enough to fly away for a few more hours. In the meantime, all the cicada can do is hope it remains unseen by potential predators.

Nearby, a **pūriri moth** is also emerging into the air for the first time. Unfolding its lush green wings, the pūriri moth also waits under the cover of darkness for its wings to dry. After years of living as a caterpillar inside the wood of a tree, it is time to search for a mate.

Crawling among the tree branches are **stick insects** that take no notice of the transformation of these winged creatures. Equally unaware of the activity above is a **kōura**, or **freshwater crayfish**, in a creek at the bottom of the bush-lined valley. The kōura has spent the night foraging while being alert to the presence of hungry **longfin eels**. After a successful night feeding, the kōura nestles into a dark space under a muddy ledge to rest out of the brightness of the coming day.

The cicada and pūriri moth have both survived the dangerous night — their wings are now dry enough for them to take flight. They have flown away, leaving only the cicada's empty shell and a hole in the tree bark that leads to a tunnel where the pūriri moth caterpillar lived before its transformation.

Cicada | Kihikihi

While it is rare to see a flying cicada, it is very common to see the empty shells of cicadas attached to tree trunks in the summer months. And you always know when cicadas are hatching as the distinctive hissing noise is unmistakable. Cicadas live underground as wingless nymphs for three or more years before making the climb up a tree trunk. Once they get high enough, they shed their skin, or moult, for the last time. This occurs regularly underground as their outer covering becomes too tight, but once they emerge with wings for the first time, they do not moult again. Cicadas live for a few weeks and suck tree sap through a straw-like proboscis.

FUN FACT Male cicadas are the loudest insects in the world — in Africa and America cicadas have been recorded at over 105 decibels.

Pūriri moth | Pepetuna

Like all moths, pūriri moths spend the longest part of their life as caterpillars. Unlike other moths, however, the pūriri larvae live under the bark of trees, and not just pūriri trees, although that is a common habitat. Pūriri caterpillars venture outside at night and feed on the callus, or scar, around the entrance to their tunnel. After more than five years living inside the tree, it's time for the large caterpillars, up to 100 mm long and 15 mm in diameter, to transform into a chrysalis. And after another few months in the tree, they hatch into their winged form, which is typically bright green or flecked with brown. Unlike the caterpillar, pūriri moths have no mouth and eat nothing during the two days they spend flying around looking for a mate.

FUN FACT The female pūriri moth is the largest of New Zealand's thousands of moths and can have a wing span of up to 15 cm across.

Stick insect | Rō

Stick insects are masters of camouflage. They often look like their host plants and when they stand still are sometimes impossible to see. Their disguise comes in different colours and textures — from smooth green to knobbly dark brown. There are over 20 different species and the biggest in New Zealand are typically 15 cm long. Mostly inactive during the day, they roam at night searching out their favourite leaves to eat. Stick insects hatch from eggs as tiny versions of adults and they moult as they grow. The eggs are laid in summer and hatch in the following spring/summer, but the insects don't usually live through the winter.

FUN FACT Some female stick insects can lay eggs without a male. They only lay female eggs, however.

Longfin eel | Tuna

Slow-growing longfin eels have an interesting life cycle. Found only in New Zealand freshwater rivers and streams, they can live up to 100 years old and grow to 2 m long. When adult eels are ready to breed they swim thousands of kilometres to the northern South Pacific Ocean, where they mate for the only time. Soon, after releasing their eggs, they die. Their eggs hatch into larvae that float with the ocean currents back to New Zealand, which become huge numbers of tiny transparent glass eels, moving to estuaries around New Zealand in spring. They then transform into grey-brown eels, called elvers, that swim up into freshwater rivers and lakes. Their final home is a long way from the ocean. Here they hide under river overhangs and logs and feast on insect larvae, kōura and fish at night. Even small birds are prey.

FUN FACT No obstacle is too high for a young longfin eel (elver). In their quest to get to their final destination, some have been known to slither over 40 m upwards over rocks and streambeds.

FUN FACT Kōura have a hard exoskeleton which they need to shed regularly as they grow. They absorb calcium from their outer shell before they moult, and then recycle the rest by eating it.

Freshwater crayfish | Kōura

Kōura prefer waterways with little or no flow, where they hide away during the day under a riverbank, or amongst fallen logs and boulders. Their bright red eyes are often all you see as they are very well camouflaged. Under the cover of darkness, they move about scavenging for food. They feed off insects, larvae and leaves. They have two larger pincers which they use to grab food, but they also wave them around if they sense danger. These pack a painful pinch. There are two species living in New Zealand waterways — smaller northern kōura grow up to 70 mm long, while the southern species are a little bigger (80 mm).

At dawn, the call of a **weka** fills the air. A squeaky *coo-ee* sound signalling the beginning of another day. Other birds add their own song to the morning chorus — the tūī's woody tones; the high-pitched *chip-chip-chip* of the **fantail**; the kākāriki's laughing song; and the musical call of the **kōkako**.

It's a noisy start to another day in the bush. A wake-up call for the daytime animals and a reminder to nocturnal animals that they should now be safely hidden away. After a good night's hunting, a **brown gecko** returns to a tree hollow inside a protected bush area. There are no rats or other introduced animals that could attack it. Going the opposite way is a **green gecko** that is just starting its hunting. The green gecko climbs high into the tree branches and begins to feast on insects and nectar.

As the sun rises further into the sky, the birds start to feed. Kōkako hop along branches eating berries and leaves at the top of the trees. Weka wander along the edge of the bush, probing the ground for worms and insects, fallen seeds and berries. Weka share the grasslands with **takahē** who tear out grasses with their strong feet and **pūkeko** who stay close to the edge of a pond where they pluck insects and vegetation from the ground.

An energetic fantail follows the ground birds. It sweeps low to catch insects that are disturbed by their movements. Its flight is jerky as it spins and turns, trying to catch insects mid-air. Successful, it flies to a nearby tree and waits until it is time to fly once more.

Gecko | Mokopirirakau

Brown forest geckos can quickly change their skin colour to blend with the surroundings. They search out insects at night to prey on and also consume fruits and nectar. While the majority of geckos are most active at night, the common green gecko forages in trees and bushes during the day. If a gecko is grabbed by its tail, the muscles in its tail spasm and pull the bones apart until the tail 'drops off'. The gecko then escapes while the predator is distracted by the still twitching severed tail. All geckos have folds of skin under their feet that allow them to walk over almost any surface, and even upside down. Geckos in captivity live a long time — the forest gecko can live 20–30 years and Duvaucel's Gecko, New Zealand's largest brown gecko, lives more than 40 years. Unlike most geckos in other countries, New Zealand's geckos give birth to live babies and forest geckos often have twins.

New Zealand has over 100 lizard species, including both skinks and geckos that only live in New Zealand. Telling them apart is easy if you know how.

Is it a gecko or a skink?

	Gecko	Skink
Head	Wide and flat	Narrow and pointed
Mouth	Wide	Small
Toes	Fat	Slender
Skin	Loose and velvety	Scaly, smooth and shiny

FUN FACT Geckos don't have eyelids and 'lick' their eyes to keep them clean.

FUN FACT Our New Zealand fantail is unique to us, but is part of a bigger family with similar birds all around the world.

Fantail | Pīwakawaka

Anyone who has walked in the New Zealand bush will most likely have seen a fantail. This tiny songbird has a distinctive fan-shaped tail that is as long as their body. The length of the tail feathers allows them to change direction in mid-air quickly and quietly. They flit and dart about trying to capture insects in and around trees, on the ground and in the sky. They follow other birds and walkers to catch the insects that are disturbed by their movements. They will also fly around to disturb insects themselves. They lay up to five eggs at a time and do this many times during the season. So even though predators take their eggs, a few usually survive each year. Because of this, the fantail is one of the lucky New Zealand birds that is not endangered.

Weka | Woodhen

Weka are flightless birds that can adapt to almost any environment, from the coast to the sub-alpine mountains and the forest in between. Weka mostly eat invertebrates and fruit, but they will eat almost anything, such as chitons on the seashore, lizards, rodents, other birds' eggs and food scraps. If they find something they can't eat, or are unsure of, they will carry it back to their nest. Because of this, they have a reputation as thieves, especially of shiny things. They lay one to three eggs typically and, although the female does most of the incubation, the male is an involved parent. There are four different subspecies of weka and some of them are under threat of extinction.

FUN FACT Weka are known to poop a lot. It is claimed that in a single day a weka produces the same amount of poop as they weigh.

Kōkako

There used to be two kōkako — the North Island kōkako with its blue wattle and the South Island kōkako with an orange wattle. While the North Island kōkako is endangered, sadly its southern cousin is considered extinct. Kōkako are poor fliers and spend their days hopping along branches in the forest canopy feeding off fruit and leaves. Occasionally they feed on moss, flowers and nectar and will sometimes prey on insects, especially when feeding their chicks. Male and female kōkako pair for life and their chicks hatch after 50 days of incubation by the female. Kōkako have a beautiful song, which has been described as similar to eerie organ music.

FUN FACT Male and female kōkako sing together in morning duets that may last for an hour and are believed to be the longest of any songbird in the world.

Takahē

Takahē are the much bigger relatives of the pūkeko. In fact, with a height of 50 cm and 3 kg in weight, it's the largest living member of its family of birds. Unlike pūkeko who live in large family groups, takahē tend to live in pairs and are territorial. Their territory is large tussock grassland that may be near a forest or in mountainous areas. In the wild, they live for 16–18 years (longer in sanctuaries) but they have one mate for life. Flightless takahē wander about pulling out the grass at the roots and eating seeds if available. Although they have no natural predators, other than introduced stoats, takehē were nearly extinct. Now they are successfully bred in captivity and released into safe sanctuaries, where they are monitored through radio antennae (see picture right). Takahē take a long time to mature to breeding age, so increasing their numbers is a slow process. Currently, the population increases by about 50 per year.

FUN FACT After 50 years with no sightings, takahē were considered extinct until Dr Geoffrey Orbell and his friends reported seeing one in the Murchison Mountains in 1948.

Pūkeko | Swamp hen

Pūkeko live near swamps and waterways and prefer open grassy areas, but you do see them at the edge of the bush. They live on all of New Zealand's main islands and the Chatham Islands. They can be found at sea level and up to 2000 m elevation. These territorial birds have few predators, and even though they can fly and swim, they tend to run away when disturbed. They eat grass and shoots of small plants, and annoyingly also pluck out garden vegetables and crop plantings with their strong bills. They also prey on small animals such as frogs, lizards, fish and small birds. Pūkeko are social animals and live in complex groups. They nest in tussock or grass clumps and all the females lay their eggs in the same nest. The males then take turns to incubate the eggs for 3–4 weeks. Even the raising of chicks is shared, with all adults and older siblings helping to feed the new chicks.

FUN FACT Pūkeko only arrived in New Zealand about 1000 years ago from Australia. But they have been here so long that most people now think of them as native.

It's the middle of the day and the sun is high in the summer sky that is buzzing with life. A **tūī** is hopping between harakeke, or flax, collecting nectar from the open flowers. Pollen sticks to the feathers of its head. The tūī spreads pollen from flower to flower, and from plant to plant, as it dips its beak into each open bud.

Honeybees are collecting nectar from the flowers of a nearby nīkau palm tree. The bees travel back and forth from their hive on the edge of the bush many times. They too spread the pollen that collects on their bodies and legs.

In the clearing where the bee hives are is a small pond where a **dragonfly** is zooming just above the water surface trying to catch the aquatic insects that hover there. The dragonfly rests on a fence post in between its energetic flights.

Entwined with the old wire fence are wild blackberry plants that have attracted **copper butterflies**. The butterflies flutter between these and other flowering native plants.

Another tūī, or perhaps the same one, lands on a nearby pōhutukawa tree to feed on the nectar of the red spiky flowers. The honeybees join in and, once again, the hot still air is filled with a happy and busy buzz.

12:00-16:00

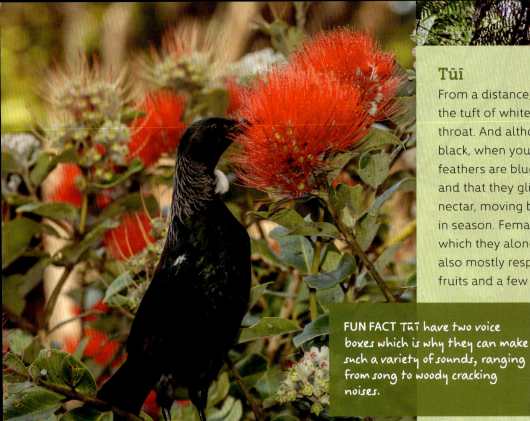

Tūī

From a distance, you will recognise the tūī by the tuft of white feathers on the front of its throat. And although the tūī's feathers appear black, when you get close, you will see its feathers are blue, green, brown and black and that they glisten. Mostly, tūī feed on nectar, moving between the different flowers in season. Female tūī lay two to four eggs, which they alone incubate. The female is also mostly responsible for feeding its chicks fruits and a few insects. Tūī are noisy and boisterous birds that protect their patches by dive bombing other birds that enter their domain. Their flight is fast, acrobatic and noisy.

FUN FACT Tūī have two voice boxes which is why they can make such a variety of sounds, ranging from song to woody cracking noises.

Dragonfly | Kapokapowai

Dragonflies have two distinct phases to their lives — the first part as larvae, or nymphs, without wings and the second phase when they transform into their flying form. Dragonfly larvae mostly live in water, but the larvae of the largest of our New Zealand dragonflies, the bush giant dragonfly, live in tunnels on the banks of streams. After a few years as nymphs, they emerge at night and shed their outer shell. Their large wings make them agile fliers. The yellow and black bush giant dragonfly is easily recognised — its body is up to 86 mm long and its wingspan is up to 130 mm. Dragonflies feed on insects, including cicadas.

FUN FACT Water-dwelling dragonfly larvae suck water into their bottoms and squirt it out to propel themselves through the water at high speed.

Honeybee | Pī honi

New Zealand has 28 species of native bees and, of those, 27 species live nowhere else. The imported honeybee arrived in New Zealand in 1939. Now there are many more honeybees than native bees and they compete with each other for the same pollen and nectar. Unlike the imported honeybees, native bees do not make honey and while honeybees live in large communal groups in wild and commercial hives, native bees do not. Making honey is a slow process. The first worker bee gathers nectar and stores it in a second 'honey' stomach, before flying back to the hive and passing it into the mouth of a second worker bee who chews it. The chewed nectar passes from worker bee to worker bee until most of the water has been lost and the nectar has been transformed into honey which is stored in the wax honeycomb. As the number of honeybees increase each year, the native bee population suffers. Both are critical to the health of the forest as they spread pollen as they forage.

FUN FACT Honey takes a long time to make. It takes eight bees all their life to make a single teaspoonful.

Common copper butterfly | Pepe para riki

Copper butterflies are native to New Zealand and live on the edges of bush areas and are also found in tussock and sand dunes. Like other butterflies, they start life as a green caterpillar with a dark red line along their backs. Their transformation starts in a chrysalis that is attached to the underside of leaves. They can be found sitting on the small-leafed pōhuehue vine or blackberry flowers and their main predators are wasps. New Zealand has over 60 butterfly species and about two thirds are not found anywhere else. Copper butterflies shouldn't be confused with the very common orange butterfly, the monarch (pictured below). Monarch butterflies flew across the Pacific Ocean over 100 years ago and are common in New Zealand gardens and their wing pattern is very distinct. They are also the largest of New Zealand's butterflies.

FUN FACT Common copper butterflies live for 1-2 weeks once they emerge from their chrysalis.

16:00 – 20:00

A pair of **kererū** sit high in a pūriri tree. In between picking off the fleshy fruit, they preen themselves and survey their territory. The seeds of a nearby nīkau palm are ready to eat. Suddenly, one swoops low and chases away another kererū that has flown into its clearing. But the new bird takes no notice and lands anyway. The kererū that stayed behind hops up to the newcomer and noisily lets the stranger know it is not welcome. The returning bird's wings are heard — *thwup, thwup* — just before it lands heavily on the tree. Fruit are shaken to the ground. Finally, the newcomer flies away and the kererū pair return to their favourite branch. They preen and watch.

The afternoon air is filled with happy chattering and flashes of bright green as **kākāriki** fly through the clearing. They circle the pūriri tree but land in a nearby harakeke plant. Clinging to the swaying flower stems, they pick off the small black seeds. The kererū pair ignore the excited parakeets. They preen and watch.

A much larger and much noisier parrot arrives. The **kākā** briefly lands on a nearby fence before flying to the top of the tallest tree. Perched in the forest canopy, the kākā is king of the bush. Far away in the southern beech forests, the kākā's relation, the **kea**, is keeping watch over its territory. There are many walkers in the forest, and the kea loiters, ready to jump onto stray objects the humans leave behind. Food hopefully, but trinkets are equally as good. The track takes the walkers through the beech forest to a mountain lookout where the views of the forest are astounding. While the humans' backs are turned the kea fiddles with their belongings.

Kererū | New Zealand wood pigeon

With a stark white breast and colourful purple and green plumage, kererū are easily recognised as the heaviest and largest of the birds flying through the bush. They are noisy in flight and when feeding in trees. When flying, the strength of their wings is evident in the sounds they make. As they move amongst the trees picking off fruit, seeds and leaves, their weight shakes, and sometime breaks, the smaller branches. Kererū have a really important role to play in the forest — they spread the seeds of trees through their poop. Since New Zealand's bigger birds are extinct, only the kererū is large enough to eat the fruits of tawa, karaka, taraire, miro and pūriri so these trees depend on the kererū for their survival. Although once hunted as food, kererū now thrive throughout New Zealand's native bush, despite only laying a single egg each spring.

FUN FACT Kererū are one of the largest pigeons in the world, weighing in at 650 g on average.

Kākāriki | Red-crowned parakeet

Kākāriki are the smallest of New Zealand's native parrots but easily recognised by the bright green feathers and red head band. They nest in holes in trees, in crevices, and in rocky nooks. There are several species of kākāriki, of which the red-crowned parakeet is one of the largest. They feed on berries, seeds and insects and are often seen foraging for food on the ground. Females lay between five and nine eggs at a time but not all of these chicks survive as the chicks feed on the ground before they can fly, where they are at risk from rats, cats and other introduced predators. Because of this, these colourful parrots are at risk of extinction and only usually seen on off-shore and predator-free islands.

FUN FACT Kākāriki is a Māori word that translates as 'little parrot'.

Kea

Kea can be found throughout the South Island. Although they live in the forest mostly, they have been seen from sand dunes to mountain tops. Kea nest in hollows and cavities on the forest floor — in between rocks, in the hollows of trees, and even just a small hole in the dirt. Males and females breed in the same pairs for many years and typically lay four eggs that take 22–24 days to hatch. The chicks are fed by their mother for three months while they stay in the nest and at this time they are at risk of introduced predators, such as stoats and rats. They eat almost anything, including plants and animals, and are legendary scavengers. They will tear strips off dead animals such as deer and sheep and have been known to dig into the backs of living sheep. But before the settlement of New Zealand, they would have foraged for plant shoot and leaves, fruits and seeds, insects and huhu grubs.

FUN FACT
The kea is the only parrot in the world to live in alpine areas.

Kākā

Kākā are relatively uncommon now, but in the past they gathered in noisy and social groups. These days, their numbers are much smaller — the Chatham Island kākā is extinct, the South Island kākā is vulnerable and the Northern Island kākā is at risk. This is mostly because they nest in hollows of trees where there is no escape from introduced predators like stoats and rats, and possums that target their eggs. There are also fewer females because they are attacked while sitting on their nest. All of the kākā's food is tree-based. They work their way through the forest seasons by eating the flower nectar, the ripe fruit, and then the seeds of the native trees. They also feed on tree sap and dig out invertebrates from the wood of the trees.

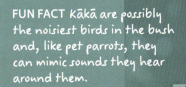

FUN FACT Kākā are possibly the noisiest birds in the bush and, like pet parrots, they can mimic sounds they hear around them.

Parrots of New Zealand

New Zealand has three parrots that look similar, but are very different to other parrots, since they separated millions of years ago. Most people think the kākāriki is a little parrot, but it is actually a parakeet. Kākāpō are large nocturnal flightless parrots and are easy to distinguish from our other two native parrots, the kākā and kea.

Which parrot is that?

	Kākā	Kea	Kākāpō
Location	Forests, North and South Islands	Alpine South Island	Off-shore islands
Flight	Yes	Yes	No
Active	Day	Day	Night
Colour	Brown-green all over	Orange beneath its wings	Bright green all over
Bill	Thick and short	Pointed and thin	Wide and large
Status	Endangered	Common	Endangered

As the sun leaves the sky, it is dark on the forest floor. The nocturnal animals of the bush are awake and venturing out of their day-time hideouts. The familiar sounds of the **ruru**, or **morepork**, fill the still air. They call to each other across the tree canopy while surveying the forest for movement with their huge eyes.

A **huhu beetle** is attracted to the moon as it arises. The shimmer of the flying beetle's wings is seen by the ruru who swoops suddenly and silently. Grabbing the unsuspecting huhu beetle with its talons, the ruru has broken its day-time fast.

Nearby, a tiny **snail** inches its way up a tree trunk. With luck, it will make it to the canopy and hide amongst the leaves before the ruru is ready for another meal. It passes very close to the outer edge of the tunnel-shaped web of a **spider**. The spider is waiting deep inside the tunnel of silk and will pounce on any animal that gets close enough. But not tonight. Tonight, the snail avoids the spider's trap and continues its climb to the canopy.

Far below on the forest floor, a **kiwi** has emerged from its burrow. The kiwi is searching for its first meal, probing the leaves and soil with its long beak. A **millipede** scurries away just in time. Safe for now. But it clambers into the pathway of a **tuatara** that is waiting silently beneath a log having just ventured out for a night-time prowl.

The day-time fast has ended and a night-time feast has begun.

20:00-24:00

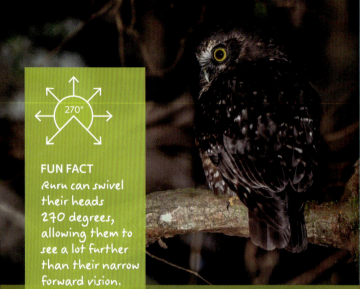

Tunnel-web spider

This native spider is one of New Zealand's largest. Their bodies grow to about 20–25 mm in length. They build their elaborate silky tunnels in the hollows of trees, around rocks and fallen logs and branches. Sitting deep inside, these spiders rarely emerge from their tunnels other than to attack food that comes close. When an insect gets too close, it triggers the silk fibres to alert the spider, which then pounces and presses its fangs into the prey to immobilise it. Its bite is not harmful to humans.

FUN FACT Tunnel-web spiders live in the deep recesses of their tunnels and usually only come out to find a mate.

270°

FUN FACT
Ruru can swivel their heads 270 degrees, allowing them to see a lot further than their narrow forward vision.

Ruru | Morepork

Ruru are small owls that have large talons and strong beaks that they use to capture their prey, which may be insects, spiders, moths, even small birds and rodents. Ruru are able to quietly stalk their prey as their wing feathers have soft feathery tips, which reduces wind turbulence. They lay up to three eggs in nests in hollows of trees, or even just a hole in the earth. The female sits on the eggs, while her mate finds and brings her food. Because the nests are often low lying, the female and the newly hatched ruru are often attacked by stoats and possums.

Kiwi

Everyone knows what a kiwi looks like, but few have seen one in the wild. This is partly because they are endangered and also because they come out under the cover of darkness to probe the ground for insects and invertebrates to eat. Kiwi are shy, unusual birds. They have tiny wings and cannot fly, they have whiskers like a cat to help them find food, and their feathers are long and loose and more like fur than other birds. Kiwi mate for life, and each season lay a single large egg. The kiwi egg is largest of all birds in relation to its body size. There are five different species of kiwi in New Zealand and some are close to being extinct, such as the Haast tokoeka. The entire kiwi population is decreasing because of predators like rats, cats and stoats that take the chicks, and dogs that kill adult kiwi.

FUN FACT Kiwi are the only birds that have nostrils at the end of their bills. They use them to find food.

Millipede

These scavengers crawl across the forest floor in search of dead and decaying leaves and fallen wood, as well as the fungi and bacteria that grow on them. Millipedes are an important part of a healthy forest-floor ecosystem as they help decomposition. They are slow moving and easily caught by their predators. The millipede's body is made up of segmented sections and covered with a hard exoskeleton. When threatened, they roll into a spiral with only their hard exoskeleton exposed. They also emit a stinky fluid to repel would-be attackers. Millipedes are typically smaller than closely related centipedes, which can grow to 25 cm long. Centipedes are also much more aggressive and can deliver a venomous bite.

FUN FACT Millipede is Latin for 'a thousand feet' and centipede translates to mean 'a hundred feet' but millipedes don't usually have 1000 legs and centipedes often have more than 100.

Is it a millipede or centipede?

	Millipede	Centipede
Length	Up to 4 cm	Up to 25 cm
Body	Round	Flat
Legs	Two pairs per segment	One pair per segment
Movement	Slow	Fast

Tuatara

Tuatara are very rare primitive reptiles that are believed to be the only surviving member of their animal family. They also only live in New Zealand. They are often described as 'living fossils' because they haven't evolved much since their dinosaur ancestors who lived hundreds of millions of years ago. They are the giants of New Zealand's reptiles, growing up to 80 cm long and weighing over 1 kg, but tuatara grow slowly. Tuatara can live to be 100 years old, and are at least 10 years old before they can breed. Their eggs are slow to hatch — it takes about a year for the tiny replica reptiles to emerge. Tuatara are also slow movers and have been predated to near extinction by introduced pests such as rats. At night, tuatara prey on insects, spiders and worms, and even small birds and eggs. During the day, they hide in hollows, under logs and even in the burrows of seabirds in coastal locations.

FUN FACT Tuatara means 'peaks on the back', which relates to the spines running along their backs.

Huhu beetle | Tunga rere

The largest beetle in New Zealand is the huhu beetle. The beetles are active at night and very attracted to lights, which is why they are often seen around houses. The larvae, known as grubs, live inside rotting or dead wood for two to three years, before emerging as winged beetles between November and March. Inside the tree, they feed on wood pulp and chew their way through the inside of trees. Like other animals that transform from a caterpillar to a flying insect, huhu larvae enter a pupa stage for about 25 days inside the tree before they chew their way out and emerge with wings. The flying beetles only live for two weeks and don't eat during this time. The female lays eggs on dead or decaying trees before it dies.

FUN FACT Māori call the grub huhu and the beetle tunga rere.

Snails | Ngata

Snails have a coiled shell for protection and their shells range from one to 100 mm across. Most land snails feed on fungi and decaying leaves, with the exception of our biggest snails. Aptly named giant snails and kauri snails, they grow to 90 mm across and are carnivores. They eat earthworms, slugs and even other snails. These giants of the snail world are now endangered and rare to see, but there are still many hundreds of smaller snails to find amongst the debris on the ground. There are over 1400 different snails and slugs in New Zealand and many of them live only here.

FUN FACT All New Zealand snails and slugs have both male and female reproductive organs but still need another snail to fertilise each other's eggs.

Glossary

Antennae — pair of long, mobile organs that are used to detect movement, smell or touch.

Bill — the pointed part of the bird's mouth (also known as the beak) that is used for probing and picking up food, preening feathers, gathering and moving objects (like twigs and seeds), pecking and fighting, and feeding chicks.

Birdsong — the musical sound of one or more birds.

Breast — the area beneath the bird's head leading to its abdomen.

Camouflage — the ability of an animal to change colour or appearance in order to blend in with its surroundings. It is used as a defense tactic allowing the animal to hide from potential predators.

Captivity — keeping animals in a confined area and not allowing them to roam completely freely. In some cases this is done to protect a threatened species.

Caterpillar — the larval stage of an insect before it changes into another shape (such as a butterfly or moth).

Chick — the name for a young or baby bird.

Cocoon — a silky case that protects larvae, or caterpillars, as they transform into their next stage.

Complex Group — a group of animals (which may or may not be related to each other) that live together for common benefit.

Complex shape — 3D shape that can't be described easily like simple shapes can.

Exoskeleton — a hard shell that supports and protects an animal's body.

Grub — another word for the larvae of certain insects (similar to caterpillar).

Incubate — the process of keeping eggs warm and alive before they are ready to hatch.

Insect — small creature that has three body parts (head, thorax and abdomen), six legs and two antennae on its head.

Invertebrate — animal that does not have a spine (backbone).

Larvae — the immature form of an animal that may or may not look like the adult.

Moult — the process by which some animals discard their hard outer shell (exoskeleton) in order to grow bigger.

Morning chorus — the loud sound of many birds singing at the dawn of a new day.

Nocturnal — mostly active at night-time.

Nectar — a sugar that is produced by a plant, which attracts insects who drink it and spread it as pollen.

Nymph — the smaller and younger form of an insect.

Pest — a destructive animal or insect that preys on other animals or plants leading to loss of habitat and animal numbers.

Plumage — the feathers that cover the skin of birds.

Pollen — a protein produced by plants that is essential to producing fruit.

Predator — an animal or fish that hunts and eats another animal or fish.

Prey — an animal eaten by another animal (a predator) as food.

Radial lines — the lines that arise at the centre of a circular web and fan outwards (like the spokes on a bicycle wheel).

Reptile — air-breathing, cold-blooded, animals that have a spine and are covered with scaly skin.

Sanctuary — a place where animals are protected from pests.

Scavenger — an animal that feeds on dead or decaying animals and plant matter.

Sibling — a relation that shares the same parents (like a brother or sister).

Territorial — Way of describing animals that protect their habitat and scare away intruders (with sounds or smells).

Index

Bee 3, 18, 21
    Honeybee/Pī honi 18, **21**
    Native bee 21
Brown gecko 13, **14**
Bush cockroach, native/Kokoroihe 4, **7**
Butterfly 7, 18, 21
    Common copper butterfly/
    Pepe para riki 18, **21**
    Monarch butterfly **21**
Centipede 3, **29**
Cicada/Kihikihi 3, 8, **9**, 10, **34**
Cockroach, native bush /Kokoroihe 4, **7**
Dragonfly/Kapokapowai 18, **20, 36**
Duvaucel's gecko **35**
Eel, longfin/Tuna 8, **11**
Fantail/Pīwakawaka 3, 13, **15**
Flax/Harakeke 18, **19**, 23
Freshwater crayfish/Kōura 8, **11**
Gecko/Mokopirirakau **12**, 13, **14, 35**
    Brown gecko 13, **14**
    Duvaucel's gecko **35**
    Green gecko **12**, 13, **14**
Green gecko **12**, 13, **14**
Ground wētā 4, **5**, 6
Harakeke/Flax 18, **19**, 23
Honeybee/Pī honi 18, **21**
Huhu 3, 25, 26, **31**
    Huhu beetle/Tunga rere 3, 26, **31**
    Huhu grub/Huhu 25, **31**
Kākā 23, **25**
Kākāpō 25
Kākāriki/Red-crowned parakeet 13, 23, **24**, 25
Kea 23, **25**
Kererū/New Zealand wood pigeon **2**, **22**, 23, **24**, 35

Kiwi 26, **28**
Kōkako 13, **16**
Longfin eel/Tuna 8, **11**
Millipede 26, **29**
Mokopirirakau/Gecko **12**, 13, **14**
Morepork/Ruru 26, **27**, **28**
Moth/Pēpepe 3, 4, **7**,8, **10**
Native bee 21
Native bush cockroach/Kokoroihe 4, **7**
New Zealand wood pigeon/Kererū **2**, **22**, 23, **24**
Ngata/Snail 26, **31**
Nursery-web spider 4, **6**
Orb-web spider **6**
Parakeet, red-crowned/Kākāriki 13, 23, **24**, 25
Parrots 13, 23, **24, 25**
    Kākā 23, **25**
    Kākāpō 25
    Kea 23, **25**
Pēpepe/Moth 3, 4, **7**, 8, **10**
Pepetuna/Pūriri moth 3, 8, **10**
Pī honi/Honeybee 18, **21**
Pigeon, New Zealand wood /Kererū **2**, **22**, 23, **24**
Pōhutukawa **1**, 18
Pūkeko/Swamp hen 13, **17**
Pūngāwerewere/Spiders 3, 4, **6**, 26, **28**
Pūriri moth/Pepetuna 3, 8, **10**
Pūriri tree 23
Red-crowned parakeet/Kākāriki 13, 23, **24**, 25
Rō/Stick insect 8, **10**
Ruru/Morepork 26, **27, 28**
Skink 14
Spiders/Pūngāwerewere 3, 4, **6**, 26, **28**

Nursery-web spider 4, **6**
Orb-web spider **6**
Tunnel-web spider 26, **28**
Snail/Ngata 26, **31**
Stick insect/Rō 8, **10,**
Swamp hen/Pūkeko 13, **17**
Takahē 13, **17**
Tree wētā 4, **6**
Tuatara 26, **30**
Tūi **1**, 13, 18, **19, 20**
Tuna/Longfin eel 8, **11**
Tunga rere/Huhu beetle 3, 26, **31**
Tunnel-web spider 26, **28**
Weka 13, **15**
Wētā 3, 4, **5, 6**
    Ground wētā 4, **5**, 6
    Tree wētā 4, **6**

About the authors

As a child, **Darryl Torckler** was fascinated by sea creatures. His bedroom walls were covered by his drawings of them and he made his first book about the sea when he was at primary school. His first photographs were taken on a Box Brownie camera during Sunday drives with his family. As a teenager, he decided to become a professional photographer and began to photograph landscapes and animals. Darryl's photographs have appeared in magazines and books and won many awards all over the world. Over the years, he has learned how to approach animals without scaring them. He's worked out how to light his subjects and the best time of day and conditions to take photos. He has learned how to take photos in dark forests and how to capture images of fast-moving animals.

Gillian Torckler was that annoying kid in class who always asked 'why?'. That curiosity led to a career in science and she still loves to explore new ideas and learn new facts. She also loves exploring the bush at night. Armed with only a bright torch, Gillian regularly goes looking for the animals that come out at night. She writes all kinds of books, but she particularly enjoys writing fact-based books, like this one.

Together, Gillian and Darryl have created 12 books for both adults and children. Many feature New Zealand wildlife, and the habitats in which they live. The Torcklers' house is surrounded by native bush and many of the pictures in this book were taken around their home.

FAVOURITE MOMENTS
One of Darryl and Gillian's favourite moments was when they first found a cicada emerging from its shell. During the day they had seen many empty shells. They waited, at midnight, near one of these trees hoping a fresh cicada might appear. The first night, they watched an empty shell for a couple of hours! Another night, a cicada climbing a tree saw them and quickly turned around and crawled back into the ground. The third time, with Gillian providing soft lighting, they watched as the cicada slowly emerged.

Exploring the New Zealand Bush

Exploring the bush at any time is good — day, night, rain or sun — the bush is always interesting. The bush has different layers and habitats. The ground that is covered with leaves and broken tree branches is home to many small invertebrates. Shrubs and climbing vines provide dense habitats for many animals. And the tree trunks lead to leafy branches where birds make their homes. When exploring the bush, patience is needed. As you walk through the bush, the animals in the ground will sense your footsteps, and the birds above will hear them. Some will follow you, like the curious fantail, but many will fly or scurry away to safety. However, if you stay still, the animals will feel safe again and begin to move about. If you don't make sudden movements or shout out, you can quietly observe as the bush comes alive. A healthy bush environment is critical for a healthy world.

FAVOURITE MOMENTS
During the daytime, Darryl and Gillian enjoy watching tūī and kererū flying through their garden.

Preparing for your bush walk

- Wear sturdy shoes or gumboots.
- Stick to a track and plan your journey so you don't get lost.
- Wear sunblock and a hat.
- Don't annoy the animals and take all your rubbish with you. Take nothing from the bush and leave only footprints.
- Obey all rules about cleaning your shoes and not taking dogs into some bushy areas to protect the animals and plants that live there.
- Visit your local protected bush area and see how healthy the bush can be when predators are controlled.

Text copyright © Gillian Torckler, 2020
Photography © Darryl Torckler, 2020
Typographical design © David Bateman Ltd, 2020

Published in 2020 by David Bateman Ltd
Unit 2/5 Workspace Drive, Hobsonville, Auckland 0618, New Zealand
www.batemanbooks.co.nz

ISBN 978-1-98-853837-2

This book is copyright. Except for the purpose of fair review, no part may be stored or transmitted in any form or by any means, electronic or mechanical, including recording or storage in any information retrieval systems, without permission in writing from the publisher. No reproduction may be made, whether by photocopying or by any other means, unless a licence has been obtained from the publisher or its agent.

The authors assert their moral right to be identified as the authors of this work.

Photography by Darryl Torckler unless otherwise noted.
Book design: Alice Bell
Printed in China by Everbest Investment Limited